Negotiating Skills

About the series

Your Personal Trainer is a series of five books designed to help you learn, or develop, key business skills. Fun, flexible and involving (and written by experienced, real-life trainers), each title in the series acts as your very own 'personal fitness trainer', allowing you to focus on your own individual experience and identify priorities for action.

Assertiveness	1 904298 13 3
Stress Management	1 904298 17 6
Interviewing Skills	1 904298 14 1
Negotiating Skills	1 904298 15 X
Time Management	1 904298 16 8

Negotiating Skills

by Astrid French

First published 2003 by
Spiro Press
17-19 Rochester Row
London SW1P 1LA
Telephone: +44 (0)870 400 1000

© Astrid French, 2003

© Typographical arrangement, Spiro Press, 2003

ISBN 1 904298 15 X

British Library Cataloguing-in-Publication Data.
A catalogue record for this book is available from the British Library.

Library of Congress Cataloging-in-Publication. Data on file.

All rights reserved. No part of this publication may be reproduced, stored in a retrieval system or transmitted, in any form or by any means, electronic, mechanical, photocopying, recording and/or otherwise without the prior written permission of the publishers. This book may not be lent, resold, hired out or otherwise disposed of by way of trade in any form, binding or cover other than that in which it is published without the prior written permission of the publishers.

Astrid French asserts her moral right to be identified as the author of this work.

Series devised by: Astrid French and Susannah Lear
Series Editor: Astrid French

Spiro Press USA
3 Front Street
Suite 331
PO Box 338
Rollinsford NH 03869
USA

Typeset by: Wyvern 21 Ltd, Bristol
Printed in Great Britain by: Cromwell Press
Cover image by: Business Today
Cover design by: Cachet Creatives

Contents

Introduction vii

How to use this book xi

Fitness Assessment 1
Test your current skills fitness

Preparation 5
1 Thinking about what *you* want 5
2 Thinking about what *they* want 6

The negotiation process 7
3 Opening the negotiation 7
4 The bargaining stage 9
5 Closing the negotiation 10
6 Tricky tactics 11

People skills 11
7 Listening and questioning 12
8 Handling emotions 13
9 Communicating confidently 13
10 Building rapport 14

Fitness Profile 17
Strengths and weaknesses identified

Preparation 21
1 Thinking about what *you* want 21
2 Thinking about what *they* want 21

The negotiation process 22
3 Opening the negotiation 23
4 The bargaining stage 24

5 Closing the negotiation   25
6 Tricky tactics   25

People skills   27
7 Listening and questioning   27
8 Handling emotions   27
9 Communicating confidently   27
10 Building rapport   28

How fit are your negotiating skills?   31

Warm-up   33

Work-out   35
Activities and exercises to build your fitness

Preparation   39
1 Thinking about what *you* want   39
2 Thinking about what *they* want   45

The negotiation process   47
3 Opening the negotiation   48
4 The bargaining stage   49
5 Closing the negotiation   55
6 Tricky tactics   56

People skills   58
7 Listening and questioning   58
8 Handling emotions   62
9 Communicating confidently   65
10 Building rapport   74

Keeping Fit   77

Further Reading/Resources   83

Introduction

Welcome to *Negotiating Skills*, part of a series – **Your Personal Trainer** – that offers you an exciting new way to learn, or develop, key business skills. Fun, flexible and involving, each title in this series acts as your very own 'personal fitness trainer', allowing you to focus on your individual experience and identify priorities for action.

Designed as a self-development workbook, each title creates an individual record of what you have achieved.

This book focuses on developing your *negotiating* skills, a key skill for success at both work and home. It gives you the opportunity of assessing where you are now, and opens doors for where you might like to go, or be, in the future. It will help you find new and more productive ways of relating to people and situations.

Everyone is capable of becoming more skilled and confident at negotiation. However, tactics and strategies, though important, are not enough. This book sees negotiation as part of building better work and personal relationships with the objective of obtaining agreements that will last, rather than 'beating' or 'outsmarting' the other party.

> *WATCH OUT FOR YOUR TRAINER*
> *He will give you tips and alert you to potential problems as you work your way through the book.*

Becoming 'fit' in negotiating may well be challenging. The ideas and exercises in this book may be a little uncomfortable at first. However, by keeping an open mind and putting in some practice, the skills of negotiating will become part of your everyday responses to situations and help you gain confidence in achieving results that satisfy both you and the other party.

What is negotiation?

We could call a negotiation a 'conversation with a purpose'.

To be more specific, the *Collins English Dictionary*'s definition is: 'A discussion set up or intended to produce a settlement or agreement'.

You may not be aware that many of the conversations you have with colleagues, customers, your manager, friends and family are a form of negotiation. Whether it is asking for a pay rise, getting a colleague to cover the telephone for you or deciding what time the kids should go to bed, we have all been negotiating since we became old enough to disagree with our parents. We've been doing it for years – so why do we get anxious when it is labelled 'negotiating'? Well, maybe because we associate negotiating with conflict – winning or losing. And you may find that you're often on the losing side.

Instead of approaching negotiations as a battle with winners or losers, you could see negotiations as involving two parties, each with a problem that needs to be solved. By taking a *collaborative* rather than a competitive approach to negotiation you attempt to find a solution satisfactory to *both parties* – both sides feel like winners.

So, what do you gain by taking a collaborative approach to negotiations?
You gain:
✓ improved relationships
✓ a better chance of building trust and respect
✓ self-confidence
✓ more enjoyment
✓ less stress
✓ more satisfactory results.

And what do you gain by taking a non-collaborative approach?

You gain:

the other party losing which leads to:
- ✗ a deterioration in the relationship
- ✗ loss of trust and respect
- ✗ loss of the chance to negotiate successfully with them.

or

the possibility of you losing which leads to:
- ✗ loss of self-confidence
- ✗ more stress
- ✗ failing to achieve your objective.

So, are you prepared to change your approach from battling to win your initial position, or making big concessions under pressure, to genuinely looking for more creative ways where a 'win-win' outcome can be achieved?

If so, read on…

This is a book for anyone who wants to improve their negotiating skills and have some fun while doing so! Whether developing your negotiating skills from scratch, or brushing up on what you already know, enjoy your read, and enjoy the benefits of becoming a better negotiator.

How to use this book

This book has been produced in a flexible format so you can maximize your individual potential for learning. You will have to put some work into it, but you should have some fun along the way.

The book is divided into four main parts:
Fitness Assessment
Fitness Profile
Work-out
Keeping Fit.

Fitness Assessment consists of 10 individual assessments. These assessments are grouped into three key skills areas or sections:

Preparation
The negotiation process, and
People skills.

The assessments offer a range of questions, exercises, choices of behaviours and attitudes to test your current skills fitness.

Try and be as candid and objective as possible when completing this part so that you have a realistic idea of your current 'fitness' in negotiating skills. And remember, there are no right or wrong answers, only feedback!

Fitness Profile gives you the results of your Fitness Assessment. It helps you to understand your responses and identify both personal strengths and weaknesses/areas for development.

Work-out offers a range of practical activities, key concepts and tips to improve your skills and help you become super-fit at negotiating.

Keeping Fit reminds you of the importance of practising your skills and allows you to develop a personal fitness plan.

You will get the best out of this book if you work through it systematically, checking up on your negotiating skills from 1-10. This will enable you to get a good overall view of your fitness.

However, you may choose to focus on a particular area of the skill (eg The negotiation process), working through the relevant sections in Fitness Assessment then moving on to subsequent sections in Fitness Profile and Work-out. These sections are clearly marked in the text, with directions to follow-up reading *at the end of each section*.

Finally, if you want a quick review of key learning points, check out the summary checklists at the end of each section in Work-out.

Whichever way you choose to use this book, enjoy the experience!

Fitness Assessment

Fitness Assessment

Fitness Assessment has been designed to test your current skills fitness.

If you want an overall picture of your skills fitness (which is recommended) you need to work through all 10 assessments and then move on to the subsequent parts – Fitness Profile, Work-out and Keeping Fit.

*If, however, you don't have time to work through all the assessments, or wish to focus your learning, you can concentrate on those sections which develop a particular aspect of the skill, and then only work through relevant subsequent sections. If you do this, make sure that you work through **all** the assessments within the individual sections.*

Assessments 1-2 focus on **Preparation**
Assessments 3-6 on **The negotiation process**
Assessments 7-10 on **People skills.**

So, let's test your current skills fitness.

Preparation

The first stage of negotiation is preparation. In order to negotiate effectively you first need to do some homework. Your confidence will be badly shaken if the other party has information or figures that show your case to be inaccurate or incomplete. Skilled negotiators tend to do more preparation than unskilled ones.

The following two assessments focus on this critical stage of negotiation.

ASSESSMENT 1: THINKING ABOUT WHAT *YOU* WANT

There is little point entering into a negotiation unless you know what you want to get out of it. You need to know what you want, and what you are prepared to concede in order to achieve an acceptable outcome.

> **TRAINER'S WARNING**
> *Don't forget to answer these questions honestly. Say what you do at present, not what you think you ought to do – make sure you get a true picture of your fitness.*

> **TRAINER'S TIP**
> *Feel free to change the genders or personnel in any of the examples offered; you may find this helps you relate to the situations.*

How well do you prepare yourself for negotiations? Look at the following statements then circle your response (either 1, 2 or 3 as described in the key below).

KEY
1 = Rarely
2 = Sometimes
3 = Always

Before entering a negotiation
1 I have a clear objective.   1   2   3

2	I have gathered all the facts.	1	2	3
3	I know what I don't want/am not prepared to accept.	1	2	3
4	I know what my interests are.	1	2	3
5	I know what concessions I am prepared to make.	1	2	3
6	I have a variety of options that satisfy both parties' interests.	1	2	3
7	I have a 'walk-away alternative' if the negotiation fails.	1	2	3
8	I know what they think about me.	1	2	3
9	I prepare myself mentally for a positive outcome.	1	2	3

Now add up your total score   SCORE

ASSESSMENT 2: THINKING ABOUT WHAT *THEY* WANT

Not only do you need to think about what you want out of the negotiation, you also need to think about the other party. How well do you know the people you are going to negotiate with? Knowing who they are, what they want and how they are likely to behave is going to help you handle the negotiation more successfully.

How well do you prepare for the other party? Look at the following statements; circle either 1, 2 or 3 as described in the key below.

KEY
1 = I rarely do this
2 = I sometimes do this
3 = I always do this

Before entering a negotiation
1. I make educated guesses about what they want out of the negotiation.   1   2   3
2. I attempt to identify, as much as is possible, their interests/concerns.   1   2   3
3. I discover their strengths and weaknesses.   1   2   3
4. I think about their 'walk-away alternative' if the negotiation fails.   1   2   3
5. I find out as much information as possible about them.   1   2   3

Now add up your scores   SCORE

Ideally, you should work through all 10 assessments to get an overall view of your negotiating skills 'fitness'. If, however, you wish to focus on improving your preparation ➡ Preparation Fitness Profile p.21.

TRAINER'S WARNING

Don't forget to answer these questions honestly. Say what you do at present, not what you think you ought to do; make sure you get a true picture of your fitness.

The negotiation process

The following four assessments focus on the actual negotiation process – from opening to closing.

ASSESSMENT 3: OPENING THE NEGOTIATION

How you open the negotia-

TRAINER'S TIP

Feel free to change the genders in any of the examples offered; you may find this helps you relate to the situations.

tion can set the tone and flavour for the whole negotiation. Remember that it's hard to shift people's first impression of you. Be conscious at the start of making the right impression.

What is your approach to opening negotiations? What is your mindset, what is your attitude to relationships? Look at the list of statements below then tick the appropriate response (either A, B or C).

1   Mindset
    A   My mindset when I enter the negotiation is to win at all costs. Negotiations are about winners and losers. ☐
    B   I have a collaborative/problem-solving mindset when I enter the negotiation. I want both parties to feel they have achieved something. ☐
    C   I am usually worried when I enter the negotiation because I fear there may be conflict, which I don't like. ☐

2   Relationships
    A   I believe relationships are very important in negotiations so my aim is not only to achieve my objective but also to maintain a good working relationship with the other party. ☐
    B   I tend to be overly concerned with not upsetting people which means I tend to make big concessions that I am later unhappy about. ☐
    C   Relationships aren't important. What matters is achieving your objective. ☐

3   Opening the negotiation
    A   I believe the best way to start a negotiation is by stating my position firmly, even if I'm bluffing, to show the other side I'm no pushover. ☐
    B   I don't have any clear idea how to start, it just happens. ☐

C I start the negotiation in a constructive way by getting agreement on the issues and identifying interests and needs. ☐

ASSESSMENT 4: THE BARGAINING STAGE

This is the stage in negotiations where there is movement, where concessions and 'trades' are made.

Look at the list of statements below. Circle the response ('Seldom', 'Sometimes' or 'Often') that most applies to you.

1 I show that I am keen to solve problems by creating options that will satisfy both parties' needs.

   Seldom   Sometimes   Often

2 Even though I am firm about achieving my interests, I also remain flexible about how those interests might be achieved.

   Seldom   Sometimes   Often

3 I recognize that because negotiating is a process of give and take – trading – I give what is high value to them, low cost to me.

   Seldom   Sometimes   Often

4 When trading I only give something if I get something back in return, even if this is an intangible benefit.

   Seldom   Sometimes   Often

5 I understand the benefit of summarizing so I do this regularly throughout the negotiation.

   Seldom   Sometimes   Often

6 I listen for verbal signals from the other party that may lead to movement or agreement.

Seldom　　　　　　　Sometimes　　　　　　　Often

ASSESSMENT 5: CLOSING THE NEGOTIATION

This is the stage where you finalize the agreement.

How do you close negotiations? Look at the following questions then circle either 1, 2 or 3 as described in the key below.

KEY
1 = I seldom do this
2 = I sometimes do this
3 = I often do this

When closing the negotiation do you
1	Summarize what you believe everyone has agreed and check it's correct?	1	2	3
2	Write down what has been agreed in detail?	1	2	3
3	Ensure both sides get measurable benefits from the agreement?	1	2	3
4	Attach timescales to the delivery of benefits?	1	2	3
5	Agree what will happen in the case of any future problems or issues?	1	2	3

Now total up your score　　　　　　　SCORE

ASSESSMENT 6: TRICKY TACTICS

Some negotiators use tactics to put you at a disadvantage in order to get what they want. These include bluffing, aggression and using threats. You need to be aware of tactics the other party may use, and know how to handle them. We will look in more detail at the types of tactics people use, to get an advantage, in Work-out.

What is your approach to tricky tactics? Look at the statements below; tick the statement that most applies to you.

A   I find it difficult to handle tricky tactics used by the other party.   ☐
B   I use tricky tactics to gain a psychological advantage.   ☐
C   I confront people who use tricky tactics.   ☐

Ideally, you should work through all 10 assessments to get an overall view of your negotiating skills 'fitness'. If, however, you wish to focus on the stages in the negotiation process ➡ The negotiation process Fitness Profile p.22.

TRAINER'S WARNING

Don't forget to answer these questions honestly. Say what you do now, not what you think you ought to do – make sure you get a true picture of your fitness.

People skills

Negotiations involve two things – people and issues. We often get so bound up with the issues that we forget about the people. How you handle people during the negotiation will affect their perception of you, and could make or break the deal. These final four assessments will

TRAINER'S TIP

Feel free to change the genders or personnel in any of the examples offered; you may find this helps you relate to the situations.

look at some of the key skills you will need to develop in order to come across more effectively with people in negotiations.

ASSESSMENT 7: LISTENING AND QUESTIONING

Two essential skills if you really want to understand the issues and underlying interests and build relationships are being able to listen and to ask the right questions. Most of us like to think of ourselves as good listeners. However, once the other person disagrees with us, or we feel quite emotional about what is being said, it's amazing how we lose our ability to listen.

Look at the following six statements. Circle either 1, 2 or 3 as shown in the key below.

'Open' questions encourage people to give more information. 'Closed' questions usually elicit a straightforward 'Yes' or 'No' response.

KEY
1 = Rarely
2 = Sometimes
3 = Usually

1	My body language shows I am listening.	1	2	3
2	I listen not just to the words but to the feelings behind the words.	1	2	3
3	I clarify to check facts, content and meaning.	1	2	3
4	I listen with empathy.	1	2	3
5	I know when to ask 'open' or 'closed' questions.	1	2	3
6	I ask questions to encourage the speaker to expand on their views.	1	2	3

Now add up your total score   SCORE

ASSESSMENT 8: HANDLING EMOTIONS

You may feel anxious about negotiations. There may be many pressures on you to succeed. However, while you may experience a range of emotions during the course of a negotiation, there are things you can do to stop them overwhelming you.

How do you handle your emotions during a negotiation? Check out the following questions then circle either 1, 2 or 3 as described in the key below.

KEY
1 = I seldom do this
2 = I sometimes do this
3 = I often do this

During the negotiation do you

1	Manage your feelings so they are expressed appropriately and effectively?	1	2	3
2	Stop yourself from taking the other party's behaviour and comments personally?	1	2	3
3	Keep cool under attack?	1	2	3
4	Respond not react?	1	2	3

Now add up your scores

SCORE

ASSESSMENT 9: COMMUNICATING CONFIDENTLY

If you feel anxious about a negotiation this could affect the way you look and sound. People will make a judgement about you, positive or negative, based on what they see and hear. If you look and sound confident during the negotiation, people will not only believe that you are confident but also that you are competent.

How confident are you in negotiations? Look at the following statements then circle the response ('Seldom', 'Sometimes' or 'Often') that most applies to you.

1 I am aware of the impact of non-verbal communication when negotiating.

   Seldom   Sometimes   Often

2 I ensure my body language matches what I'm saying.

   Seldom   Sometimes   Often

3 My behaviour is assertive rather than passive (appeasing) or aggressive.

   Seldom   Sometimes   Often

4 I can control my negative, inner dialogue.

   Seldom   Sometimes   Often

ASSESSMENT 10: BUILDING RAPPORT

Rapport is the ability to relate to others and build a climate of respect and trust; the ability to see the other person's point of view, even if you don't agree with it. Maintaining rapport is essential to ensuring that the negotiation goes well.

> **ASSERTIVE BEHAVIOUR**
> *Assertive behaviour is about being honest, open, direct and focused. It is about asking for what you want or need, while recognizing others' needs.*

> **PASSIVE BEHAVIOUR**
> *Passive (or appeasing) behaviour is about withholding your true feelings, trying to please others, feeling insecure about your relationships, role or job.*

Look at the following questions. Circle the appropriate response (Yes or No).

Do you
1 Know how to build rapport
  easily with others?   Yes   No
2 Match your style to the other
  person's?   Yes   No

Ideally, you will now have completed all 10 assessments and tested your overall skills fitness. If so ➡ Fitness Profile p.17.

If, however, you have chosen to focus on developing your people skills ➡ People skills Fitness Profile p.27.

Fitness Profile

Fitness Profile

Well done, you've gone through Fitness Assessment – now you can find out the results!

Fitness Profile allows you to evaluate your current skills fitness – your strengths, weaknesses and priorities for action. It builds up into a fitness profile unique to you.

Fitness profiles 1-2 relate directly to assessments 1-2. Similarly, profiles 3-6 and 7-10 relate directly to assessments 3-6 and 7-10.

Fitness Profile 21

Preparation

Profiles 1 and 2 will help you build up a picture of how well you prepare – a key element of effective negotiation.

PROFILE 1: THINKING ABOUT WHAT *YOU* WANT

Look back to assessment 1 (p.5) and make a note of your score here SCORE

> For assessment 1, the higher your score the better you understand what you want to get out of a negotiation.
> The **maximum** score is **27**.
> The **minimum** score is **9**.

PROFILE 2: THINKING ABOUT WHAT *THEY* WANT

Look back to assessment 2 (p.6) and make a note of your score here SCORE

> For assessment 2, the higher your score the better your understanding of the methods and motivations of the other party in a negotiation.
> The **maximum** score is **15**.
> The **minimum** score is **5**.

So how healthy is your preparation? Add together your scores for assessments 1 and 2 to give your **total preparation score:** TOTAL PREPARATION SCORE

The higher your total score the better your approach to preparation.
The **maximum** score is **42**.
The **minimum** score is **14**.

Congratulations, you recognize the importance of preparation and apply yourself accordingly. You are skills fit.

You are moderately fit. You have an understanding of the importance of preparation but some areas need improvement – focus on these in Work-out.

You are not skills fit! You may have been hard on yourself or you may have identified some key areas that you will need to focus on in Work-out.

Ideally, you should work through all 10 assessments, profiles and work-outs to improve your overall fitness. However, if you have chosen to focus on improving your preparation ➡ Preparation work-out p.39. Before doing this, however, it is a good idea to do some quick mental preparation ➡ Warm-up p.33.

The negotiation process

Profiles 3-6 will help you build up a picture of how well you handle the various stages of the negotiation.

PROFILE 3: OPENING THE NEGOTIATION

Look back to p.8 to remind yourself of the statements in assessment 3, and how you responded. Make a note of the options you ticked below.

	A	B	C
1 (Mindset)	☐	☐	☐
2 (Relationships)	☐	☐	☐
3 (Opening the negotiation)	☐	☐	☐

1 For the first set of statements the preferred response is **B**, 'I have a collaborative/problem-solving mindset when I enter the negotiation. I want both parties to feel they have achieved something.' This is positive in approach and promotes a 'win-win' outcome ➡ **3 POINTS**

2 For the second set of statements **A** is the preferred response – 'I believe relationships are very important in negotiations so my aim is not only to achieve my objective but also to maintain a good working relationship with the other party.' Relationships are important and need to be maintained positively during, and beyond, any negotiation

➡ **3 POINTS**

3 'I start the negotiation in a constructive way by getting agreement on the issues and identifying interests and needs' (**C**) is the preferred response. Again, it is conducive to a 'win-win' outcome ➡ **3 POINTS**

TOTAL ASSESSMENT 3 SCORE

> For assessment 3 the higher you score the better you are at opening negotiations positively.
> The **maximum** score is **9**.
> The **minimum** score is **0**.

PROFILE 4: THE BARGAINING STAGE

Look back to p.9 in Fitness Assessment; remind yourself of the statements and your responses. Make a note of your responses below.

	Seldom	Sometimes	Often
1	☐	☐	☐
2	☐	☐	☐
3	☐	☐	☐
4	☐	☐	☐
5	☐	☐	☐
6	☐	☐	☐

Now add up your score. Give yourself 1 POINT for 'Seldom', 2 POINTS for 'Sometimes' and 3 POINTS for 'Often'.

TOTAL ASSESSMENT 4 SCORE

> For assessment 4, the higher your score the greater your ability to achieve an acceptable outcome through bargaining.
> The **maximum** score is **18**.
> The **minimum** score is **6**.

PROFILE 5: CLOSING THE NEGOTIATION

Look back to assessment 5 (p.10); remind yourself of the questions and your responses. Write down your score for assessment 5 here **SCORE**

For assessment 5 the higher you score the more skilled you are at closing negotiations.
The **maximum** score is **15**.
The **minimum** score is **5**.

PROFILE 6: TRICKY TACTICS

Look back to p.11 to remind yourself of the statements in assessment 6 and your response. Make a note of your response (A, B or C) here ☐

For this assessment the preferred response is **C**, 'I confront people who use tricky tactics.' Tricky tactics should not be used by yourself or others! This is an open, assertive response

 3 POINTS

If you scored 3 points for this assessment you have a healthy approach to tricky tactics.
The **maximum** score is **3**.
The **minimum** score is **0**.

So how healthy is your handling of the various stages of the negotiation process? Look back to p.23 for your score for assessment 3 and write it down here ☐

Now your assessment 4 score ☐

Your assessment 5 score ☐

Your assessment 6 score ☐

Add these individual scores together to make your total negotiation process score:

TOTAL NEGOTIATION PROCESS SCORE

The higher your total score the better you are at handling the various stages of the negotiation process.
The **maximum** score is **45**.
The **minimum** score is **11**.

 Well done, you have developed a collaborative negotiating style and appear to be comfortable handling negotiations.

 You are quite fit, but some areas need improvement – focus on those in Work-out.

 You are not skills fit. You have identified some key areas that you will need to focus on in Work-out.

Ideally, you should work through all 10 assessments, profiles and work-outs to improve your overall fitness. However, if you have chosen to focus on the negotiation process ➡ The negotiation process work-out p.47. Before doing this, however, it is a good idea to do some quick mental preparation ➡ Warm-up p.33.

People skills

Profiles 7-10 will help you assess how well you handle people in a negotiation.

PROFILE 7: LISTENING AND QUESTIONING

Look back to assessment 7 (p.12); remind yourself of the statements and your responses. Make a note of your score here
SCORE

For assessment 7 the higher you score the better you are at listening and questioning.
The **maximum** score is **18**.
The **minimum** score is **6**.

PROFILE 8: HANDLING EMOTIONS

Look back to assessment 8 (p.13); remind yourself of the questions and your responses. Now make a note of your score here
SCORE

For assessment 8, the higher you score the better you are at handling your emotions.
The **maximum** score is **12**.
The **minimum** score is **4**.

PROFILE 9: COMMUNICATING CONFIDENTLY

Look back to p.14 in Fitness Assessment; remind yourself of the statements and the options you chose for assessment 9. Make a note of these options overleaf.

	Seldom	**Sometimes**	**Often**
1	☐	☐	☐
2	☐	☐	☐
3	☐	☐	☐
4	☐	☐	☐

For this assessment give yourself 1 POINT for 'Seldom', 2 POINTS for 'Sometimes' and 3 POINTS for 'Often'.

Now add up your total score

TOTAL ASSESSMENT 9 SCORE

For assessment 9, the higher your score the greater your ability to communicate confidently.
The **maximum** score is **12**.
The **minimum** score is **4**.

PROFILE 10: BUILDING RAPPORT

Look back to assessment 10 on p.14. Remind yourself of the two questions and how you responded (Yes or No). Giving yourself 3 POINTS for Yes and 0 POINTS for No, make a note of your score here

SCORE

For assessment 10, the higher your score the better your understanding of building rapport.
The **maximum** score is **6**.
The **minimum** score is **0**.

So how healthy are your people skills? Look back to p.27 for your score for assessment 7 and write it down here ☐

Now your assessment 8 score ☐
Assessment 9 score ☐
Assessment 10 score ☐

Add these individual scores together to make your **total people skills score**:

TOTAL PEOPLE SKILLS SCORE

The higher your total score the better you are at handling people in negotiations.
The **maximum** score is **48**.
The **minimum** score is **14**.

 Congratulations, you have excellent interpersonal skills. Keep up the good work! A review of this section in Work-out may be useful in helping you maintain your fitness level.

 You are moderately fit. You have a general understanding of interpersonal skills. You have a few areas that could use some work – focus on these in Work-out.

 Your skills are not what they should be to communicate effectively with others. However, going through Work-out and practising the exercises will improve your skills!

Ideally, you should now have worked through all 10 assessments and profiles. If so, turn to p.31 to discover your **overall negotiation skills fitness level**.

If, however, you have focused on developing your people skills ➡ People skills work-out p.58. Before doing this, however, it is wise to do some quick mental preparation ➡ Warm-up p.33.

How fit are your negotiating skills?

Ideally, you should now have completed all 10 assessments and profiles, and have a good idea of how fit you are in negotiating.

Personal fitness profile

Look back at how you scored in the three sections:
Preparation
The negotiation process, and
People skills.

Make a note of your individual total scores for these sections below:

Preparation ☐
The negotiation process ☐
People skills ☐

What is your total negotiating skills score?

TOTAL NEGOTIATING SKILLS SCORE

 Congratulations, you are fit at negotiating. Are there any areas you could improve still further?

 You are quite fit. You could do with improving your negotiating skills.

 You are unfit! You need to do some work and build your negotiating skills.

Now take another look at your individual total scores for the three sections. Circle these scores overleaf.

	UNFIT	**REASONABLY FIT**	**FIT**
Preparation	14-23	24-33	34-42
The negotiation process	11-22	23-34	35-45
People skills	14-25	26-37	38-48

Are you strong or weak in any particular section or skills area? Are you, for example, strong at preparation but weak at process? Or perhaps you have strengths and weaknesses across all sections? Look back at your individual scores in profiles 1-10. Can you identify any particular strengths or weaknesses?

THOSE AREAS IN WHICH I HAD THE HIGHEST SCORES (STRENGTHS)

THOSE AREAS IN WHICH I HAD THE LOWEST SCORES (WEAKNESSES)

Congratulations on your strengths, but you do need to take action to develop your weaker areas.

Before moving on to Work-out, however, you need to do some quick mental preparation ➡ Warm-up opposite.

Warm-up

'If you think you can or you think you can't you're probably right.'

It is wise to do a quick mental warm-up before tackling the exercises in Work-out.

Take a few moments to reflect on your reasons for wanting to become a better negotiator, identifying any benefits it will bring you. Now complete the following.

> **TRAINER'S TIP**
>
> *To get the most out of the warm-up you will need to be relaxed and sitting comfortably.*

Why do you want to become a better negotiator?

....
....
....

What benefits will you get?

....
....
....

Now imagine what it might be like to have what you want come true. Think of a particular negotiation in which you might be involved in the near future; imagine that you have just *successfully* completed this negotiation.

What do you see? (Look around you, take in the details.)

....
....
....

> **TRAINER'S TIP**
>
> *The more vividly you can imagine yourself achieving your goal the more your unconscious mind will believe it is true and will programme you to act accordingly.*

What do you look like?
My eye contact is ....
My body posture is ....
My hands are ....

What do you sound like/what are you saying?
The tone of my voice is ....
I am saying ....

How are others reacting [positively] to you?
Others are saying ....
Others are being ....

How are you feeling?
I am feeling..

You are now ready to make this a reality. If you have completed all 10 assessments and profiles ➡ Work-out p.35. If, however, you have chosen to focus on a particular skills area/section

  Preparation work-out p.39
  The negotiation process work-out p.47
  People skills work-out p.58

Work-out

Work-out

You have now completed your Fitness Assessment, identified your strengths and areas on which you need to work. Now it's time to get fit!

Packed with practical exercises and activities, Work-out contains all the equipment you need to become super-fit at negotiating.

Look back at your personal fitness profile on p.31-32. Where do your strengths and weaknesses lie? Do they lie in certain areas of the skill – are you, for example, generally strong when it comes to preparation but weak when it comes to handling process? Or do they relate to all three skills areas? Depending on your personal fitness profile, you can either focus on improving a particular area of skill or work on individual weaknesses within each area.

Of course, if you want to raise your level of performance in all areas then complete all the activities; then you really will be super-fit!

Work-outs 1-2 relate directly to profiles 1-2. Similarly, work-outs 3-6 and 7-10.

Preparation

'Fail to prepare, prepare to fail.'

Many people think they can walk into a negotiation without having done their homework. This will put you at a big disadvantage in the negotiation and you may end up accepting offers or making concessions which, if you had done a little bit of preparation, you would not accept. Good preparation before the negotiation will give you more confidence in the negotiation and help you secure the best outcome for both parties. The following two work-outs will help you achieve this.

WORK-OUT 1: THINKING ABOUT WHAT *YOU* WANT

Have a clear objective
You need to have a clear idea about what you want and what you don't want out of any negotiation. However, this shouldn't be too rigid or be confused with a 'bottom line'. For example, if you badly need a holiday in the sun and want to go to Ibiza, but the only holiday available is Majorca, rejecting Majorca because it isn't Ibiza may mean you don't get any holiday. When thinking about your objective, focus on the problem – 'I need a holiday' – rather than the solution – Ibiza. Also knowing what you *don't* want – cold weather – will enable you to reject unsuitable offers. So make sure you truly understand your objective: 'I shall be happy if at the end of the negotiation I have [a holiday in the sun].'

Know what your interests are
When you are thinking about what you want out of a negotiation, think about *why* you want it. Underneath your defined goals and objectives you will have needs, interests, concerns, anxieties and things you care about.

For example, if you want a pay rise from your boss, your interests apart from wanting more money might be 'job security', 'possibilities for promotion', 'gaining valuable experience', 'easy access from your home', 'liking the people you work with' etc. So you might ask your boss for a pay rise of £1,000 but be prepared to settle for less money if, say, you get offered training linked to future promotion. In other words, a negotiation may be *successful* because it *satisfies your interests* although not necessarily your initial position (or what you said you wanted), ie £1,000.

Exercise 1: Identifying interests
Think of a negotiation in which you you were involved recently that was not successful.

List your interests (concerns, anxieties, things you care about)
....
....

List the other party's ....
....

Here is an example to help you think about interests. A husband and wife want to buy a new car. He wants a Porsche, she wants a Volvo estate – they can't afford both!

Husband's interests	**Wife's interests**
Image	Safety
Speed	Image
Lots of techy gadgets	Room for kids/shopping
Feel young	Reliable etc
High quality etc	

Go back to exercise 1: are there any intangible interests you hadn't thought about? (*We will come back to this example when we look at 'Options'.*)

TRAINER'S TIP

Interests can be tangible (concrete) – quality, size, money; or they can be intangible (abstract) – image, status. Intangible interests can sometimes be more powerful than tangible ones.

It may be a good idea to prioritize your interests so that when you come to think about making any concessions you can make sure they are the less important ones.

What concessions are you prepared to make?
Negotiating is about trading. If you want a win-win outcome then you will have to be prepared to give something if you want something in return. If you have prioritized your interests then it is the least important ones you may be prepared to concede.

Options that satisfy both party's interests
Before you enter a negotiation you will need to think creatively about the different ways in which you could satisfy both your and the other side's interests. Widen your horizons – don't assume there is only one solution. Going back to the husband and wife example, there could be many ways of satisfying both their interests which do not necessarily satisfy their opening positions of Porsche and Volvo. Can you think of any? How about a BMW or Mercedes estate, a Shogun, a second-hand Porshe or Volvo etc?

Now go back to exercise 1 and see if you can identify any options that satisfy both your and the other party's interests that you hadn't thought about before.

A 'walk-away alternative' if the negotiation fails
Something very rarely done but invaluable *before* you enter the negotiation is to think about what you will do if the negotiation fails. If they say 'No' to all your options, how do you walk away from the negotiation with confidence?

Let's go back to the example of asking the boss for a pay rise. If you had looked for other jobs which were paying more money and had set up some interviews, or better still, had gone for an interview and been offered a job, your hand would be strengthened in the negotiation with your boss; you know that if he didn't agree you could walk away because you had something else.

It's up to you whether you reveal your walk-away alternative to the other party – it could encourage them to rethink. If you do, make sure it doesn't sound like a threat which would damage the relationship.

If you cannot identify a walk-away alternative, then be aware that you may have to settle for less than you really need.

Gather the facts

'Information is power.' Gather facts, statistics, precedents and case histories to support your case. Imagine you were buying a second-hand car and had not researched how much cars of that age and in that condition normally sold for. Or, if you had not found out the mileage or the service history of the car, you would be going into that negotiation with one hand tied behind your back. You would be forced to believe everything the other party told you.

Trust is one of the most difficult and important aspects of negotiating. To be a collaborative negotiator you need to build trust and openness in the negotiation, but that doesn't mean you automatically have to believe everything the other party says. If you have done your homework and gathered the facts you will be in a better position to know whether *they* are being trustworthy.

When putting your case in a negotiation, printed evidence is especially potent. People are often sceptical of oral arguments, but they assume that words printed in an article or report are more likely to be true. Take the evidence into the negotiation. You may end up using very little of the material but you'll negotiate with more confidence knowing you have it available.

What do they think about you?

What is the other side's perception of you? How do they view you? Do the views they have of you strengthen or weaken your hand in the negotiation? For example, if you were negotiating with your boss they may see you as trustworthy and hardworking, which is good, but also perhaps not very assertive. You may want, therefore, to work on coming across more assertively in the negotiation.

Exercise 2: Identifying others' perceptions of you

Think about a negotiation in which you will be involved in the near future. What are the views the other party hold of you? ....
....
....

Do these views help or hinder your negotiating position?.....
....
....

What do you need to do to strengthen appropriate views and weaken inappropriate ones? ....
....
....

Prepare yourself mentally

Apart from the practical or physical aspects of preparation, research has shown that in order to stand a greater chance of achieving success it is important to prepare mentally. Successful business people and athletes do this regularly. What makes mental rehearsal so powerful is that the mind cannot tell the difference between a clear visualizing experience and reality. In situations where you need mental confidence or where you feel anxious, for example a negotiation, this works particularly well. Repeated visualization of successfully performing in a situation that normally makes you feel nervous actually builds up your self-image. It is a strong self-image that helps you look and sound confident.

TRAINER'S WARNING

Control negative thoughts. Make sure you think about what you want, not what you don't want.

Exercise 3: Visualizing success
Sit in a quiet room. Relax your body. Think of a negotiation you will be doing in the near future.

State clearly and concisely what your objective is and why you want to achieve it ....
....

Now visualize yourself achieving success. Focus on as much detail as possible:

What does the room look like? ....
....

How are you sitting? ....

Describe your body language ....
....
....

What is the other person saying and doing? ....
....
....

List the questions they are asking which you can answer confidently ....
....
....

Describe the positive feelings that go with this image ....
....
....

Part of your mental preparation is about speaking to yourself more positively. How often do you say to yourself things like 'They'll never agree to this' or 'I'm useless at negotiations'? Negative thoughts lead to negative behaviour, which leads to negative outcomes. Change the way you think about negotiations and yourself as a negotiator. Enter negotiations with an open, problem-solving mindset. See the other person as someone who has a problem to solve, just like you, not as an enemy.

WORK-OUT 2: THINKING ABOUT WHAT *THEY* WANT

Once you are clear about what you need and how you feel, you are ready to think about the other person. How well do you know the people you are going to negotiate with? What kind of relationship do you have with them?

What do they want out of the negotiation?

Put yourself in their shoes. Be objective and make an educated guess about what their objectives are. If you know the other side, this will be a lot easier. Be careful not to jump to conclusions too quickly. For example, if you were buying a second-hand car you might assume that the seller's main aim is to get as high a price as possible. In fact her aim may be to sell the car as quickly as possible to get it out of her garage. During the negotiation itself you should attempt to discover the other side's objectives.

Identify their interests/concerns

In work-out 1 you needed to think about *your* underlying needs, the reasons you want what you want. The other party's interests are no less important. You need to answer these questions to help you prepare effectively for the negotiation:
- What are the other party's concerns/anxieties?
- What do they care about?
- How does this benefit them? (Why should they agree to anything that doesn't benefit them?)

Know their strengths and weaknesses
- How experienced are they in negotiating?
- Do they have more power and resources than you do?
- Can you trust them?
- What negotiating style do they have?

The more background information you have on them the more you will know what to expect in the negotiation.

Their walk-away alternative

It may not be possible to find this out before the negotiation. If you know they have a strong alternative it may put you in a weaker position in the negotiation, but you will also have to work out how you can legitimately weaken or diminish their alternative.

Example

> *Fred's landlord wanted to raise his rent by £10 per week. Fred believed the landlord's walk-away alternative was to get another tenant if he didn't pay up.*
>
> *How did Fred weaken the landlord's position? Fred knew the landlord not only wanted more money but also a tenant that paid on time, kept the flat well maintained and wasn't a nuisance to the neighbours. Fred managed to convince the landlord to increase the rent by a much smaller amount by stating that the landlord had no guarantees that a new tenant would, like Fred, pay regularly, keep the flat well maintained etc. He also argued that it could potentially cost the landlord a lot of money in advertising fees.*

If their walk-away alternative is weak, or you can weaken it, you are in a much better position to reach a win-win outcome!

Find out as much information as possible about them (and who else may be affected by this negotiation)

Ask people who have negotiated with them before. Read any literature on their organization. Find out what would turn them on and what would turn them off.

Are they the decision maker? You may waste a lot of time negotiating with the wrong person. Check that the person you are negotiating with can actually make the decision. Not much point negotiating otherwise.

Are there other people who will be affected by this negotiation? For example, if you manage a team of people and negotiate with a member of the team a bigger pay rise than for other members of your team, you may have a revolt on your hands when the other team members find out. So the impact of your negotiation may affect more than the person sitting opposite you. During the negotiation, therefore, you may need to consider what impact any agreement you reach will have on others.

Preparation checklist

- ✓ Have a clear objective.
- ✓ Negotiating is about trading. What are you prepared to give in order to get something back?
- ✓ Gather as much evidence as you can to back up your case.
- ✓ Put yourself in the other party's shoes. See the negotiation from their perspective. How will they benefit?
- ✓ Identify who else may be affected by the negotiation.
- ✓ Have a walk-away alternative if you cannot reach agreement.

The negotiation process

The following four work-outs will help you improve your handling of the key stages in the negotiation process.

WORK-OUT 3: OPENING THE NEGOTIATION

If you enter the negotiation thinking 'I've got to win' or 'I'm going to be really tough' you have set the negotiation up to have a win-lose outcome. And you may not necessarily be the winner! This isn't war, it's a negotiation. The two parties will have some goals and interests that are similar. You differ on how to achieve those goals. If you see negotiations as two parties needing to resolve their problems then you can begin to establish a climate of cooperation, not conflict.

Separate the people from the issues

The relationship between you and the other person/party is important in negotiations but shouldn't be confused with what you are negotiating about. You need to separate the issues from the personalities. If you are very concerned about conflict, or the other side not liking you, you may have developed what is called a 'soft' negotiating style. You may find that people take advantage of you in negotiations because under pressure you go soft on the issues and make big concessions, which you later regret. By all means be positive and friendly towards the other party while at the same time being tough about working to find a solution that satisfies both parties' needs. Don't assume that by being firm on finding a solution you have to treat the people harshly. So, be firm on finding a solution which satisfies both parties' needs but handle the people carefully. This approach says: *I want to win and I want you to win too*.

Exercise 1: You and me against the problem

Next time you are in a negotiation write down on a sheet of paper the key issues you want to discuss, as if it's an agenda. Sit next to the other person and put the paper between you. This is a subtle way of saying to the other person that you or I aren't the problem, the problem is here on this piece of paper. This will move the focus of the negotiation from 'you against me' to 'me and you together against the problem'.

Focus on interests, not on positions

One of the premier sports agents in the USA, Leigh Steinberg, says he starts negotiations by saying 'Look, there are two ways we can go about this. Spend a lot of time giving speeches about our positions, or we can talk about what is really important to us here. Let me know your interests and I'll let you know mine.'

Start the negotiation by establishing rapport and mutual interests. The other side may start with an initial position; these are often extreme and unrealistic. Ignore them and focus on the other person's interests and your own goals and principles, while you generate other options.

TRAINER'S WARNING
Don't discuss solutions at this stage. Just identify and agree the issues.

For a collaborative approach to work you will need to start the negotiation by getting agreement on what the issues are.

Try to frame the issues in a neutral way. For example, if you want to discuss your workload with your boss it would be better to discuss 'the work schedule' rather than stating 'you give me too much work'.

WORK-OUT 4: THE BARGAINING STAGE

Once you have both agreed what the issues are, you can start looking at possible solutions. This is the stage in the negotiation where things start to move, and concessions and compromises are made.

Create options

The skill here is to be as creative as possible. Is there a possibility that you can achieve both what you need and what the other side needs?

Exercise 1: Creative options

Background: It is the morning of the monthly team meeting and Jane has been asked by her manager to answer the telephones instead of attending the meeting. Because Jane was not at the team meeting last year when they discussed holidays she didn't get the dates she wanted. She really wants to go to the team meeting today.

Jane's manager says he would like her to stay behind and answer the phones.

What options could Jane put to her manager? ....
....
....

(Possible options: use an answerphone, get someone else to answer the phones, Jane to attend the meeting only when holidays are being discussed etc.)

Create options based on both sides' interests

When putting forward an option in the negotiation make sure it dovetails with both parties' needs. If we go back to the previous exercise, using an answerphone may satisfy Jane's need to be at the meeting. But if her manager was worried about an answerphone giving the wrong impression to customers then this option wouldn't be satisfactory.

> **TRAINER'S TIP**
>
> *When you put forward an option beware of giving in too quickly. If you believe it's a good option for both parties then stand your ground for a bit.*

Remember that at this stage you are only discussing possible solutions, no one is ready to commit themselves yet. When putting forward options say *'What if we...'* or *'How do you feel about...?'* rather than *'We should do this...'* or *'The sensible solution is...'*. You want to demonstrate a collaborative rather than a dictatorial style. If the other side feel they are being dictated to they are less likely to agree. If the other side say 'No' to an option then ask them 'What is it you don't like?' You may well get their underlying interests which will enable you to come up with other options to meet those interests. At this stage in the negotiation you may have just one option that the other side seems happy with or you may have a number of options on the table and you are now ready to do some trading.

Trading
Negotiating is about giving and receiving – trading. You can't expect to get something from the other party if you are not prepared to give something in return. This is the bargaining phase of the negotiation. Some useful guidelines when trading:
- If we just give, we end up lose-win. If we just take, we end up win-lose.
- Only give what you feel you can afford; preferably items that are of relatively low value to you but high value to the other side.
- Seek to gain things that will be of high value to you. This may not necessarily be a tangible item, it could be a feeling, goodwill or a greater sense of security.
- Be prepared to be generous if you can see long-term benefits – as long as it feels like win-win!
- Encourage the other side to trade.

When trading, use phrases such as 'If you... then I will...'.

So, for example, 'If you increase the quantity I will consider reducing the price.'

Remember, in a negotiation that involves money you can often get bogged down in thrashing out the financial deal. Almost always, however, there will be other items that have significant value that could be traded. Having a collaborative approach to your negotiations may open up possibilities to reaching agreement that aren't solely focused on the financial.

Put forward proposals
Use the first half of the negotiation to talk about your and their interests and discuss various options. The second half of

the negotiation is about trading and putting forward proposals.

Proposals help to move the negotiation forward and can break deadlock. When you put forward a proposal, highlight the fact that you are putting forward a proposal; trade and move in stages.

Let's look at how Jane from the previous exercise might move the negotiation forward.

Jane: 'So you're not keen on any of the other options we discussed other than me answering the phones during the staff meeting.'

Manager: 'Unfortunately, we have some very important customers ringing in and I need someone with experience answering the phones while the meeting takes place.'

Jane: 'OK, so you need me to answer the phones and I need to get my holiday dates agreed. I'd be happy to *consider* manning the phones if you would agree my holiday dates with me now as I won't be able to raise them at the meeting.'

Manager: 'Yes, I might consider that.'

Jane: 'Well, I'd like to make a firm proposal then: if you agree my holiday dates then I *will* answer the phones.'

> **TRAINER'S TIP**
>
> *Trade in stages; start with 'I will consider...' and, if they agree, move to 'I will...'.*

Making agreements reciprocal ('I'll do this, if you do that') can also be effective if there is limited trust between the parties or some doubt about the other person keeping their end of the bargain.

When putting your proposals put them as a whole package, not separate items to be agreed one at a time. It can lead to a breakdown of trust if you raise a second issue only after you have agreement on the first. Remember that everything in a negotiation is tentative until the end. In other words, 'nothing's agreed until *everything's* agreed'.

Going back to our example of Jane and her manager, Jane

believed that the issues under discussion, and subsequently agreed, were:
- her answering the phones instead of attending the meeting
- her manager guaranteeing her holiday dates.

If her manager, after that agreement, decided to raise another issue, for example asking Jane to stay late to handle an important telephone call in the evening, this might well not only damage the relationship between Jane and her boss but also affect Jane's original agreement to answer the phones during the meeting.

Summarize regularly

Negotiations can be complex; it is easy to forget what has been discussed or agreed so far. Don't be afraid to summarize regularly. Summaries can help you and the other party clarify any misunderstandings or confusion and help break deadlock. Say something like:

'I'd like to summarize what I believe we have agreed so far…'

or

'So, to summarize what we've discussed so far…'

or

'Just so I understand you correctly, are you saying…'

- Check everyone agrees the summary: *'Is that correct?'*
- Frame summaries in a positive way, eg *'We both agree on x, y and z. We now need to find a way forward with a, b and c'* rather than *'We seem to be stuck on a, b and c.'*
- Use summaries to end one issue before moving on to the next.

'Hidden' signals

During the negotiation both you and the other party may be sending 'hidden' signals, either verbally or non-verbally. The real meaning of a message is in the tone of voice and body language. You don't have to read books to become an expert on body language. You will know if someone is looking relaxed and sounding interested in what you are saying or uncomfortable and disinterested. Become aware of the signals you may be sending with your body language or tone of voice. The work-out on people skills will help you on this.

Observe the other party's body language and tone of voice. If someone's body language or tone seems to be at odds with what they are saying, mention it. You may say something like 'You say you agree, but to me it looks like you are unsure. Am I right?'

Listen carfeully for the verbal signals people send. Verbal signals are non-absolute or qualified statements. Not picking up on these subtle signals may mean you miss out on the other party's willingness to move or agree.

Exercise 2: Understanding hidden signals

Verbal signals
Write down what you think these signals mean.

They say:
A 'We *might* find it difficult to…'
Which means: ....

B 'We couldn't possibly consider it *in that form*.'
Which means: ....

C 'It's not our *normal* practice to do that.'
Which means: ....

D '*At the moment*, we couldn't consider it…'
Which means: ....

E 'Our price for *that quantity* is...'
Which means: ....

F 'We would not be prepared to discuss it *at this stage*.'
Which means: ....

Answers
A But not impossible.
B Rejig it   .
C We might be prepared to make an exception.
D We might be able to at a different time.
E But for a bigger quantity...
F We might later.

WORK-OUT 5: CLOSING THE NEGOTIATION

Summarize what you believe has been agreed, who is to do what and by when. Check with the other side that they agree and write it down. Avoid vague language such as 'try harder' or 'as soon as possible'. Ensure the agreement is 'SMART' – Specific, Measurable, Achievable, Realistic and Timed. Ask specific questions to test out whether the agreement is SMART. For example, 'What exactly are you going to do?', 'How exactly?', 'When specifically?'

Depending on the type of negotiation, it is a good idea to write down or agree how you will resolve any issues or problems that may arise in the future.

If it is important to maintain or even enhance the relationship between you and the other side, then make a generous gesture at the end. Is there something you can give which the other side will appreciate but costs you little? Now is the time to

> **TRAINER'S WARNING**
>
> *Watch out for the other side wanting to raise new issues in the closing stages of the negotiation. If they want to raise new issues, then everything is open to discussion. Remember, 'Nothing's agreed until everything's agreed.'*

smoothe over any difficulties you may have had during the negotiation and start to rebuild the relationship.

WORK-OUT 6: TRICKY TACTICS

The other party may attempt to deceive or trick you. Tricky tactics can be: deliberate deception, personal attacks, positional pressure. Prepare to deal with all three. Here are some common examples.

> **TRAINER'S WARNING**
>
> *If you use tricky tactics during the negotiation you are not playing the 'collaborative game'. This could well backfire on you.*

Good person/Bad person

This is where you have two people, one playing the 'nice guy', the other playing the 'tough guy', or one person playing both parts. The tough guy frightens you into doing a deal with their 'nice' partner. This tactic exploits our natural vulnerability and our desire to be liked. Don't allow yourself to be bullied or manipulated into reaching an agreement.

'I have no authority'

This tactic allows the other side to avoid concluding the negotiation by claiming not to have the authority to agree terms. Find out the limits of the other person's authority before you start the negotiation.

Rushing

Negotiations are almost always more fruitful if given plenty of time.

Resist the other side putting the pressure on to reach agreement because of lack of time. Agree a sensible timescale at the start of the negotiation and stick to it.

Bluffing

It's not always easy to tell if someone is bluffing. It may help you decide if you have had previous experience of their style

TRAINER'S WARNING

If someone uses tricky tactics on you it will probably damage the relationship and it is unlikely you will want to negotiate with them again. Bearing this in mind, don't use tricky tactics when you negotiate.

or notice a mismatch beween their verbal and non-verbal messages.

The best way to cope with tricky tactics is to be prepared for them, not to reply in kind and to have a strong walk-away alternative. You can also recognize the tactic explicitly and this could neutralize it. For example, 'Oh, not the good guy/bad guy routine!' Alternatively, you could ignore their tactics and negotiate over them. If all that fails, walk out of the negotiation, explaining the conditions on which you would be willing to re-enter. If the other party is not interested in resuming the negotiation they were probably not interested in reaching an agreement in the first place.

The negotiation process checklist

- ✓ Enter the negotiation with a collaborative/problem-solving mindset.
- ✓ Establish mutual interests.
- ✓ Identify and agree the issues.
- ✓ Look for creative options which satisfy both sides' interests.
- ✓ Summarize regularly.
- ✓ Watch out for hidden signals either verbal or non-verbal.
- ✓ Close the negotiation with a SMART summary.
- ✓ Be prepared for tricky tactics.

People skills

When we negotiate we are often so bound up in the process of getting a good deal for ourselves that we forget that the other side are human beings, not companies or machines. We need to learn how to handle people sensitively in the negotiation while at the same time being assertive on the issues. How we handle people may well affect the outcome of the negotiation. We sometimes express ourselves in a way that is misinterpreted by others. By increasing our control over our verbal and non-verbal behaviour we can minimize the likelihood of the other party rejecting our message because of the way we expressed it. The key skills here are:

- Listening and questioning
- Handling emotions
- Communicating confidently
- Building rapport.

The following four work-outs will help you improve your people skills.

WORK-OUT 7: LISTENING AND QUESTIONING

Many people believe that to be a good negotiator you need to be a good talker – that communication primarily takes place through speaking, and that you are in control if you are doing most of the talking. However, listening and questioning are essential skills for negotiators; you cannot be a good negotiator if you don't listen and ask the right questions. How are you going to build rapport, trust and respect without listening? How are you going to understand the other side's interests, concerns and perceptions if you don't ask them questions and listen to their replies? Most people feel that listening is about waiting until the other person draws breath and then speaking. Listening is fundamentally about understanding the other person.

People feel they will lose control of the negotiation if they are not doing most of the speaking. If you believe you will lose some control by not speaking, try the following exercise with a friend.

Exercise 1: The importance of showing you are listening

1. Get your friend to speak for two minutes on their summer holiday or their hobby.
2. While they are speaking, listen very actively: give good eye contact, look interested, nod, say 'yes' and 'mm' regularly.
3. After about one minute stop looking at them, look around the room, start fidgeting, look bored. Note what happens to the speaker.
4. After two minutes, if your friend could continue that long, ask them how they felt.
5. The speaker will usually say things like '*It was almost impossible to continue speaking in the same way*', '*I lost my train of thought*' etc. They may say that they felt angry because you stopped listening, or that they felt they were boring you.

This exercise shows you the power the listener has in the communication process. If you want good quality information you need to give good quality listening.

Show you are listening

Listening effectively is not easy. You need to do more than just sit there and use your ears.

Have you ever walked into your boss's office and, while you were trying to speak to them, they were reading papers or taking telephone calls? How did that make you feel? When we are speaking we want the listener to show us that they are giving us their full attention and attempting to understand what we are saying.

How to show you are listening
- Position yourself so you can give good eye contact.
- Look interested in what the other person is saying.
- Have open body language (or you may want to mirror them – see work-out 10 on building rapport).
- Stop fidgeting.
- Nod and say 'yes' and 'mm' occasionally.
- Use words to encourage the speaker to continue.

Listen to the feelings behind the words
When people are speaking to you the words they say are only part of what they are expressing. If you pick up on the non-verbal information coming to you this will reveal how they *feel* about what they are saying. Do they look happy, sad, uncomfortable, defensive? State your perception of their feelings: 'You seem unsure about that.' Are their words saying one thing and their body language another? They may be saying 'Yes' but not giving you good eye contact and having a downcast facial expression. If you only listen to the word 'Yes' you may be missing something important. It might be a good idea to check out what you're seeing. You may say something like 'You're saying Yes to my proposition but you don't seem happy about it. Am I right?'

You may feel uncomfortable or not be used to picking up on others' feelings. However, it is better to explore how other people are feeling, and resolve any issues resulting from that, than assume you have an agreement which will not hold because the other side is feeling unhappy about it.

Clarify
Checking you have correctly understood what the other person has said, that you have picked up the facts and the meaning accurately, is fundamental to active listening. Clarify by repeating back in your own words what you think the speaker has said. Use phrases such as 'Can I just check, what you are saying is…'; 'What I understand you are saying is…'

Listen with empathy

Listening with empathy can enrich your interpersonal skills and foster relationships. You don't have to like the other person or agree with them, it's the ability to put yourself in the other person's shoes and understand where they're coming from without losing your own identity. Empathy is different from sympathy. Sympathy is feeling sorry for the other person. When you are negotiating with another person, put yourself in their shoes – attempt to see the negotiation from their perspective. If you were them, would you accept what you are proposing? What concerns or anxieties are they experiencing? Can you help to allay those fears or anxieties?

'Open' and 'closed' questions

Some questions are better at getting information than others. People often make the mistake of asking closed questions when they want information.

Ask **OPEN** questions if you want information or to find out how the other person thinks or feels. Open questions begin with 'Who', 'When', 'What', 'Where', 'How' and 'Why'.

Ask **CLOSED** questions if you want confirmation or commitment. Closed questions begin with 'Is', 'Do', 'Can', 'Have', 'Will', 'Are', 'Would' and 'Was'.

Exercise 2: Using open questions

1 Ask a friend about their holiday. You are only allowed to ask open questions.
2 Get your friend to signal every time you ask a closed question.

TRAINER'S WARNING
When asking questions ensure your tone sounds genuinely interested rather than interrogational.

Questions to encourage the speaker to expand their view

Questions can be much more effective than making statements. They can help reduce potential conflict and help you understand the other side's interests better. For example, if the other side makes a statement which you feel is inaccurate, rather than say 'You're wrong' or 'I disagree', which is likely to provoke a defensive remark, ask them 'How did you arrive at those figures?' If they say 'No' to a proposal, ask them 'What don't you like about my proposal?' Examples of questions to encourage the speaker to expand their view:

> 'What do you think...?'
> 'How specifically would you do that...?'
> 'How do you feel about...?'
> 'What's your view on...?'

WORK-OUT 8: HANDLING EMOTIONS

Emotions are a natural, integral part of our lives and influence our behaviour. If we welcome the positive aspects such as enthusiasm, motivation, joy etc we must also accept the existence of more negative feelings. A good negotiator can control their emotions no matter who is speaking to them, or whatever the subject matter or words used.

Manage your feelings

The skill is to keep your emotions in check so you can carry on listening. Your negative feelings may hamper your ability to think straight, be creative or get accurate information. It could well be that the other person may not realize they have said something or done something that has triggered negativity in you and it may be important for you to listen to them. Managing your feelings isn't the same as squashing them. Squashing your feelings can not only damage your health but also affect your ability to build rapport with the other party in a negotiation.

If we voice how we feel we can confront the issue and communicate our view: 'I feel let down that what we agreed last week is now not going to happen'; 'I feel uncomfortable with that suggestion'; 'I feel annoyed that my contribution to the report has not been acknowledged.'

Notice the above examples use 'I feel' and not 'you made me feel'. This conveys an acceptance of responsibility for your feelings and not blaming others for how you feel. This is important because not only is it true that the only person who can control your feelings is *you* but you will come across less aggressively.

Stop yourself from taking others' behaviour and comments personally

Are there people you find it difficult to listen to or who 'wind you up' (this may be for a variety of reasons: you find them aggressive, you don't like their tone of voice, you don't like the way they look etc)?

Exercise 1: Identifying emotional triggers
1 Identify those people that trigger negative feelings in you.
2 Are there topics or issues you find it difficult to listen to?
3 What words do you not like listening to? What words are 'red rags' to you?

Recognize when you are having a negative feeling and work on putting it to one side or just letting it go if it is going to hamper your ability to think and negotiate effectively. Say to yourself *'It is important I listen to this person and hear accurately what they say'*.

Keep cool under attack
The following exercise will help you manage yourself physically and respond constructively.

Exercise 2: Managing your emotions
1 Become aware of the feeling you are experiencing.
2 Name it, own it – remember no one *makes* you angry.
3 Relax – breathe in and then focus on breathing out.

4 Notice any physical signs, eg muscles tensing, teeth clenching.
5 Relax your joints and muscles.
6 Don't respond yet.
7 Notice what the other person is doing and saying.
8 Think positively, say to yourself things like 'Maybe they have had a bad day' or 'Perhaps they don't know how to express themselves better' and visualize a positive outcome.

> **TRAINER'S TIP**
>
> *Focus on your body language and tone of voice, looking and sounding calm.*

9 Ask questions and listen actively to understand exactly what the other person means or wants.
10 Focus on solving the problem, not attacking the person.

Respond not react

When we feel under attack or face hostility from others the emotional part of our brain is triggered. Our heart rate and blood pressure increase to enable us to fight or flee. In a negotiation this results in us reacting aggressively or giving in under pressure. This will not only damage the relationship but is less likely to produce a successful win-win outcome. When we react rather than respond we are not using the thinking part of our brain.

Practise the following exercise with a friend. This exercise is very effective if you are in a situation where you disagree with someone or you have opposing views which could lead to conflict. This exercise should be used in combination with the exercise above.

Exercise 3: Managing differences
1 Decide on a topic where you and a friend have opposing views.
2 Let your friend speak for a minute on her view.
3 You are to listen actively and when she has finished summarize back what you have heard. Then say 'Is that correct?' Check your summary is correct.

4 You may then need to ask some questions to clarify and ensure you really understand her position.
5 You can now put your view. You are not allowed to use the combination 'Yes, but…'. Everyone knows that the next thing said will be negative; this will stop the other person listening to you. So, instead use '**I appreciate you feel…**' or '**I agree…** (find something they have said that you can agree with)' or '**Yes, and** what concerns me is…'
6 When your friend replies, summarize back what she says.
7 See if you can create win-win by building a bridge between your view and hers.

How did you get on? How did your friend feel about having her views summarized back to her? If you did this exercise well the other person should say she felt she was really listened to and understood. You may also have noticed how there was much less emotion generated. One of the ways to control your emotional reactions is to engage your 'thinking brain'. Summarizing back what you have heard and asking questions is a powerful way of controlling your emotions and those of the other side.

WORK-OUT 9: COMMUNICATING CONFIDENTLY

First, let's debunk the myth – these's no such thing as an unconfident person. Everybody is confident in some things. Yours may be baking a cake, knitting a jumper or changing a car tyre. You have techniques, which you may be unaware of, that give you confidence in some situations. Because we are often anxious about the outcome when we negotiate, this is likely to be revealed in our body language and tone of voice. Our anxieties will stop us looking confident.

If you look and sound confident then the likelihood is that the other person will think you are confident; this will lead them to believe you are competent. What you need are techniques for looking and sounding confident when you negotiate. You will need to work on some mental as well as physical techniques. Let's start with the physical first.

Non-verbal communication – body language and tone of voice

When you communicate, as I am sure you are aware, you don't just use words, but body language and tone of voice as well. Research has shown that in face-to-face communication body language accounts for some 55% of someone's impression of you, your tone of voice for 38% and the words you actually say for only 7%. If you want to test this out for yourself, do the following exercise.

Exercise 1: The impact of non-verbal behaviour on your message

1. Say to a friend 'I am really excited about going on holiday' but say it in the following way. Make your tone flat and boring. Have a bored facial expression, drooping posture and look down.
2. If your friend isn't already laughing, ask her if she believed you were excited about going on holiday. The odds are she will say she didn't believe you. Ask 'Why not?' The answer will be because you did not look or sound like you were excited.

In other words, people make judgements about whether we are credible or not based primarily on our body language and tone of voice – not on what we say. This doesn't mean the words aren't important. The skill here is to ensure that when you are speaking your body language and tone of voice match what you are saying.

Try the exercise again. This time, when you say you are 'excited' about going on holiday, make your body language and tone of voice look and sound excited. I bet your friend believes you this time!

Imagine you are negotiating with your boss for some time off because you have been working very late. Your facial expression and tone will need to express that this is very important to you and must be taken seriously. Otherwise you may not get what you want, particularly if you look and sound apologetic.

So, ensuring that our verbal and non-verbal communication matches is a powerful way of looking and sounding confident.

Behave assertively
Behaving assertively will also help you look and sound confident. However, lots of people get confused about what assertiveness actually means. What do you think 'behaving assertively' means? Many people get confused between aggressive, passive (appeasing) and assertive behaviour. So let's explain them.

Aggressive behaviour can be described as an approach which works on the mindset 'I win and you lose'. In the aggressive style you are quite capable of stating how you feel, what you think and what you want, but it is at the expense of others' rights and feelings. You go on the attack when you don't get your way. Your non-verbal behaviour might include a clenched jaw, jutting, rigid gestures and pointing and invading the other person's personal space. Your tone may be loud and abrupt. In a negotiation you are more concerned about winning than building relationships. You may use threats and bluff to get your way. At the end of the negotiation the other side may feel bitter and exploited.

Exercise 2: Practising aggressive behaviour
Imagine you are in a negotiation and you are saying to the other person 'I'm not happy with that...':
- Sit upright and rigid.

> **TRAINER'S WARNING**
>
> *This isn't so you get good at being aggessive but so you recognize the differences between aggressive, passive and assertive behaviour!*
>
>

- Clench jaw and teeth.
- Stare at them.
- Point your finger at them whilst you speak.
- Make your tone harsh and abrupt.

How did that feel? What impact do you think that would have on the other person?

Passive behaviour can be described as an approach which works on the mindset 'I lose and you win'. It's about avoiding conflict at all costs; it's about appeasing. When you are behaving passively you don't express your true feelings, thoughts and needs directly. If you do speak up directly you make disclaimers such as 'I'm sorry but…', 'I'm most probably wrong but…'. Your body language is likely to be slouched, with your hands wringing or fiddling with hair or pen. You are unlikely to give good eye contact and may over-smile because you don't want to upset people or cause conflict. Your tone is often quiet and apologetic. Because you are not saying what you mean you don't look like you mean what you say. You often put yourself down. In a negotiation you are so concerned not to upset the other person that you are likely to give in easily under pressure and make substantive concessions, which you later regret.

Exercise 3: Practising passive behaviour
This is the same as the previous exercise, but with passive body language and tone this time:
- Sit more slouched with legs crossed.
- Avoid eye contact.
- Fiddle with your hair or a pen.
- Make your tone quiet and apologetic.

How did that feel? What impact do you think that would have on the other person?

When you communicate **assertively** you express clearly your feelings, thoughts, needs and opinions. You stand up for your rights without violating the rights of others. You can deal effectively with criticism and hostility without becoming aggressive or defensive. You are open to negotiation and securing win-win outcomes. Your body language is relaxed and open. Your posture is upright and balanced. Your eye contact is direct without staring. You convey an air of confidence and empathy. You look like you mean what you are saying. Your tone is firm but appropriately friendly. You want to aim to be firm on securing a win-win on the key issues while keeping friendly with the person.

Exercise 4: Practising assertive behaviour

Now's your chance to practise assertive behaviour:

- Sit upright but not rigid.
- If you are sitting at a desk, have one hand resting on the desktop or both hands on the desktop loosely linked. Use open palm gestures if you want to gesture.
- Keep gentle eye contact (not staring).
- Relax your face and look interested (smile only when you are genuinely pleased; don't over-smile or make exaggerated facial expressions).
- Keep your tone friendly but firm (your aim is to ensure the other person clearly understands your message but does not feel under attack).

> **TRAINER'S TIP**
>
> *Show your hands when you are negotiating, don't keep them under the desk. If we can't see people's hands we instinctively feel they are hiding something.*

How did this feel? What differences were there in how you felt between the three behaviours? I hope you felt more confident and in control when you were being assertive.

Some people say they feel silly and weak being passive. Others find it hard to come across aggressively. What is important here is that you can distinguish for yourself the differences between the three behaviours, and work on coming across more assertively.

Now we have done the non-verbals, let's look at a very useful verbal technique called the 'basic three steps'. This is helpful when you want to respond assertively to someone:

1 **Listen and acknowledge you have heard the other person.**
   You need to use the skills you learnt in the Listening work-out p.58.
2 **Say what you think, feel, need or want.**
   Use 'I think...' or 'I feel...' not 'You make me feel...'
3 **Negotiate win-win.**
   If it's appropriate, otherwise just state what you want to happen next.

Let me give you an example of using the three steps:

Boss says to Mary: 'I need this report done urgently. Would you mind staying late to do it?'

Mary: 'I can see this is wanted urgently and normally I don't mind staying late if something's urgent.

*(**Step 1:** shows she has listened and acknowledged her boss)*
However, I have made arrangements to go out tonight and it won't be possible to change them.'
*(**Step 2:** saying what she needs backed up by a good reason)*

Boss: 'That puts me in a difficult situation.'

Mary: 'I understand this is difficult for you. What if I start some of it now and get in earlier tomorrow morning?'
*(**Step 3:** Mary is negotiating here, attempting to get win-win. If her boss doesn't like that option she needs to come up with another one. If he doesn't like any of her options she either has to stick to her guns and not do it or stay late and cancel her appointment. Both options are win-lose. It would*

be far better if she could find a way to satisfy both their interests.)

If you want to initiate a discussion start with Step 2, then when the other person has replied use the three steps.

Exercise 5: Practising assertiveness
Take situations at work or in your personal life, or use one of the following suggestions:
- Someone wants you to do something for them and you don't want to do it.
- Your boss asks you to work late and you want to tell them that you genuinely are unable to do it.
- You are unhappy about a piece of work someone has done for you and want them to do it again.

If you want to know more about assertiveness there are lots of excellent books written on the subject (including *Assertiveness,* **Your Personal Trainer**), or go on an assertiveness training course.

Control negative, inner dialogue
Do you ever talk to yourself in your head? Do you have a little 'voice' that stops you doing or saying something? Is the voice positive and encouraging when you are dealing with difficult situations or is it negative and critical? For example, before you go into a negotiation, does your voice say things like 'It won't go well, they'll never agree' or 'My face will go red and it won't come out right'.

Unfortunately, most of the inner dialogue we have with ourselves is negative and very often unrealistic. We often think things are going to go much worse than they do in reality. We can persuade ourselves into the most dreadful situation in advance and, if we do it well enough, we can almost guarantee a self-fulfilling prophecy of real disaster. The world of sports discovered a way to use this kind of inner thinking in a positive way by encouraging athletes to substitute negative thoughts for positive ones – to use the inner voice as a coach not a critic.

You are more likely to achieve your goal if you focus on achieving it rather than focusing on what could go wrong. This is not saying that all you need to do is think rosy thoughts and everything will be fine. Focusing on your goal must be backed up by having done your homework and using the skills and techniques outlined in this book.

Exercise 6: Identifying and controlling negative thoughts

Think about a future negotiation. Make a list of all your typical negative thoughts ....
....
....

Note how you *feel* when you think about these negative thoughts.

Now imagine you are a professional coach and you are coaching someone about to enter an important negotiation. What positive thoughts could you substitute for those negative ones? ....
....
....

Note how you feel when you think about these positive thoughts.

Did you know that human beings are a bit like icebergs? The reason is that you only see a small part of us; most is hidden. Above the 'waterline' is what we show (our body language) and what we say (our words and tone of voice). Below the waterline are our thoughts, feelings, experiences, knowledge, beliefs, values etc. Unfortunately, for most of us, what goes on below the waterline has a nasty habit of 'leaking' above and coming out in our body language and tone of voice.

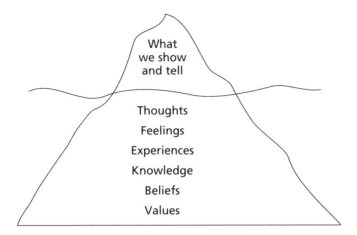

Let me give you an example of the process at work.

Suppose you are about to enter a difficult negotiation and you are:

- Thinking 'This is going to be difficult, they are not going to agree, they are more experienced than I am, I won't handle it well'. This is likely to lead to…
- Feeling anxious and unconfident. What happens now is that those feelings and thoughts leak above the 'iceberg'…
- Showing your anxiety in your body language and tone of voice. You will have a worried facial expression, not give good eye contact and have unrelaxed hand movements. Your tone is likely to be quiet and monotone.

What impact do you think this will have on the other person? Are you more or less likely to achieve your objective?

The lesson to be learned here is – change the way you think about a situation and it will change your feelings, which will change the way you come across to others.

If you are still concerned about controlling that little voice in your head, try this exercise.

Exercise 7: Keeping 'Nora' under control
1 Give the voice a name (someone you don't know), preferably a funny name. I call mine 'Nora'.
2 When you are about to enter a negotiation, if Nora is saying positive things such as 'It will go well', 'They will agree to your proposals', then listen to her.
3 However, if the voice is saying negative things and dwelling on what could go wrong then…
4 Tell them to 'get lost', 'bog off' (use your own words).
5 If a little voice is saying 'This technique will never work', that's Nora speaking to you. You know what to say…

WORK-OUT 10 : BUILDING RAPPORT

To communicate effectively with another human being you need to establish rapport.

Rapport means being on the same wavelength, feeling comfortable and 'connected' in some way with that person. There are two ways to look at the other person in the negotiation: you can choose to look for differences between you or you can choose to look for similarities. It is hard to build rapport if you emphasize differences. But if you emphasize what you have in common you are more likely to get cooperation. Rapport helps you build trust and openness in the negotiation.

We are all experts in building rapport but we often do it without realizing it. For example, if you were in a large department store and you saw a little girl crying because she was lost, how would you help her? I am sure you would bend down to match her height, soften your voice and use language she could relate to. Subconsciously you would be 'mirroring' her in order to build rapport. Have you ever been at a party or in a restaurant and watched people who were in deep conversation? They will often do a matching 'dance'. They will sit in the same way and even drink their drinks at the same time.

One way to create rapport is to match the other person's body language and tone of voice, sensitively and with respect. If they feel you are mimicking them then this will break rapport and could cause offence. Diana, Princess of Wales, was very good at building rapport. People would comment on how she would sit beside them, look and sound interested in their point of view. Is it any wonder she was called the 'People's Princess'?

TRAINER'S WARNING

Before attempting mirroring in a negotiation, practise in other situations first.

Exercise 1: Mirroring to build rapport

Sit opposite a friend or watch someone on a talkshow on the television and observe:

1 **Body language** – are they upright, leaning to one side, slouched, hands in pocket, arms folded, legs crossed etc?

   Put yourself in a similar position. If you feel uncomfortable matching them exactly you can, for example, match their crossed legs with your crossed feet. The skill here is to match sensitively and with respect to show you are not very different to them.

2 **Voice** – is it loud, quiet, slow, fast, enthusiastic etc?

   You may have noticed that certain people's tone of voice affects you more negatively than others. People who talk slowly with a quiet voice often find it difficult to build rapport with people who speak loud and fast. Don't try to change your voice completely but attempt to move nearer the other person's style.

   If you are negotiating with, say, a customer who is very angry and they are speaking in a loud, aggressive tone, don't mirror their aggressive tone or words. Start by mirroring the strength of feeling and speed of their voice.

3. **Checking you have built rapport**. Start by mirroring the other person's body language and tone of voice. Then change your body language; for example, if you were mirroring their crossed arms, uncross your arms, lean forward. If you were mirroring their abrupt tone, soften your tone and speak slower. You will know that you have established rapport if they start to mirror you. You may want to think of it like this: *If you are in step with another person, the next step you take they are likely to follow.*

People skills checklist

- ✓ How you handle people will affect the success of the negotiation.
- ✓ Show you are listening; listen to the feelings behind the words.
- ✓ Check understanding.
- ✓ Manage your feelings.
- ✓ Respond not react.
- ✓ Ensure your body language and tone of voce match what you say.
- ✓ Control negative inner dialogue.
- ✓ Build rapport by mirroring.

Keeping Fit

Keeping Fit

Congratulations on finishing the book. Hopefully you have enjoyed the experience and gained from the advice and insights offered.

As you have discovered, developing your negotiating skills will get you more of what you want out of life and enhance your work and personal relationships. But like any skill, practice makes perfect and the more times you use it, the better you get at it. You need to keep skills fit, and this is what the final part of this book is all about...

Keeping fit

As mentioned at the very start of this book, negotiation is a key skill for success both at work and home, and it is important you don't let it slip.

You need to keep on your toes, keep practising. If you feel your skills slipping then look through the book again, remind yourself of the key learning points, even run through a couple of exercises. Better still, set yourself some real-life targets *now* to keep yourself up to scratch.

Make a note of your targets in your fitness plan below. Specify actions and timescales; this will keep you focused and fit.

Personal fitness plan

Target/Action	By when	✓

Further Reading/Resources

Further reading/resources

Books

Fisher, Roger, Patton, Bruce, and Ury, William, *Getting to Yes,* Arrow Books, 1997

Goleman, Daniel, *Emotional Intelligence*, Bloomsbury Publishing, 1996

Hodgson, Jane, *Thinking on Your Feet in Negotiations*, Pitman Publishing, 1996

Videos

Everyone's a Winner, Capita Learning & Development